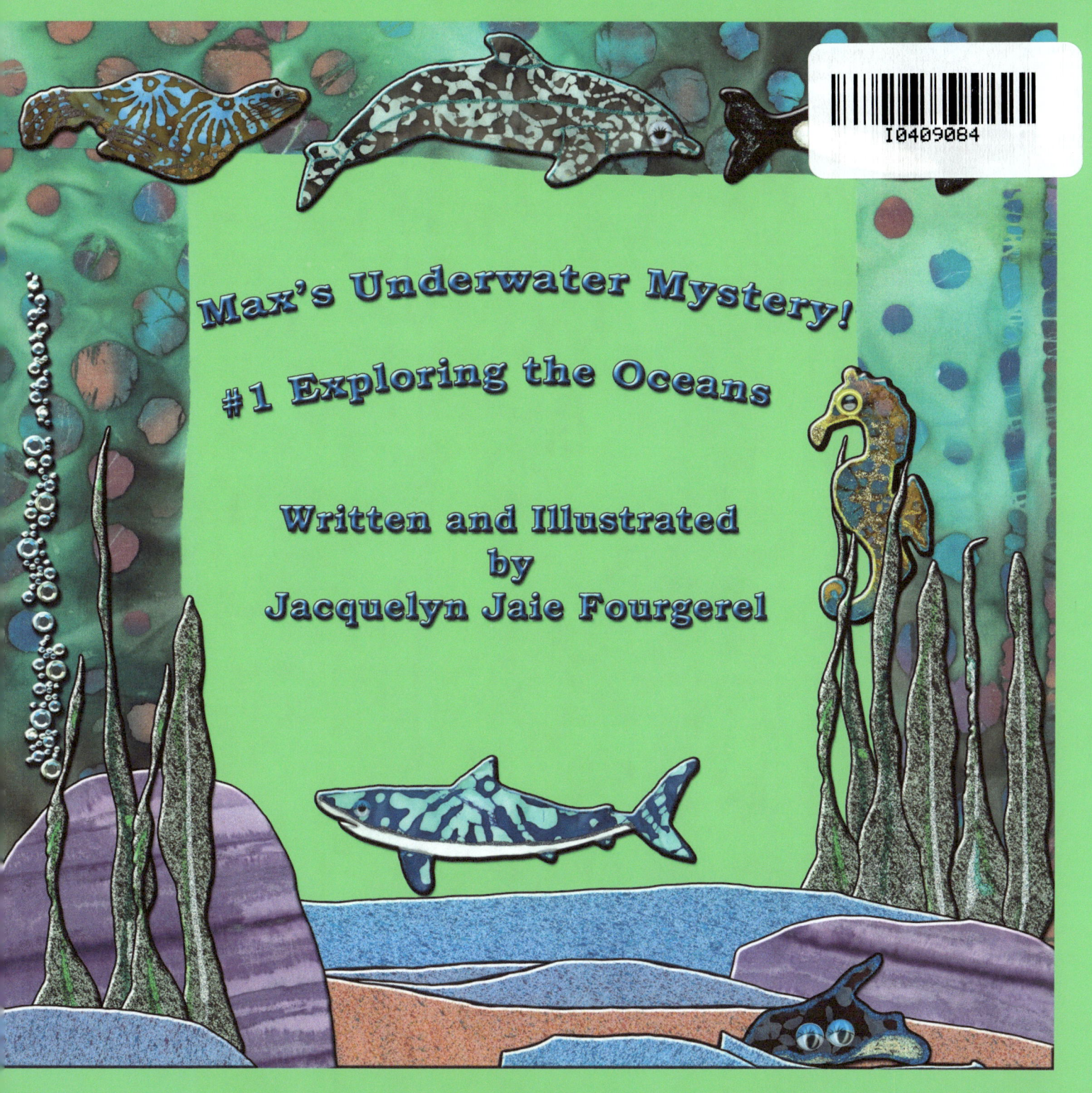

Max's Underwater Mystery!

#1 Exploring the Oceans

Written and Illustrated
by
Jacquelyn Jaie Fourgerel

"Dad, look at all of these sea creatures in the ocean with us.
What are they?
Where do they live?
How big do they get?"
Max asked.

"Out there and far beyond what our little seahorse eyes can see, are what I call underwater mysteries!"
Dad said.

"I want to find out what these underwater mysteries are!" Max thought to himself.

So, Max decided to go off and explore the sea creatures he saw from his seaweed home.

"Are you an underwater mystery?"
Max asked.

"Yes, I am an underwater mystery.
I live with 10 to 30
members of my family,
and...

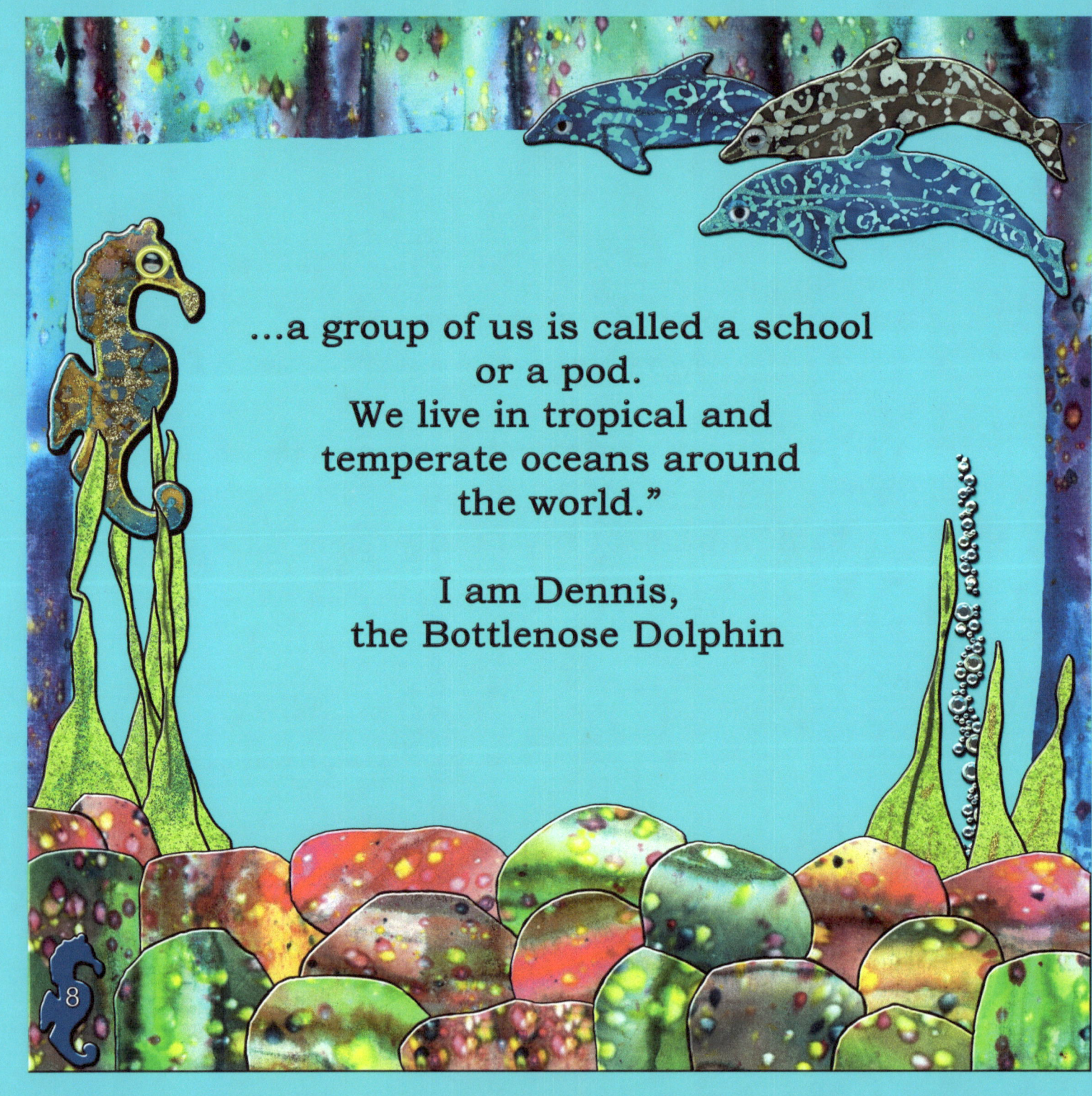

...a group of us is called a school
or a pod.
We live in tropical and
temperate oceans around
the world."

I am Dennis,
the Bottlenose Dolphin

8

9

"Are you an underwater mystery?"
Max asked.

"Yes, I am an underwater mystery.
I can swim down to 600 feet
and hold my breath for 30 minutes,
and...

... I live in all parts of the
Northern Hemisphere and
eat many different types of fish."

I am Dawn Marie,
the Harbor Seal.

13

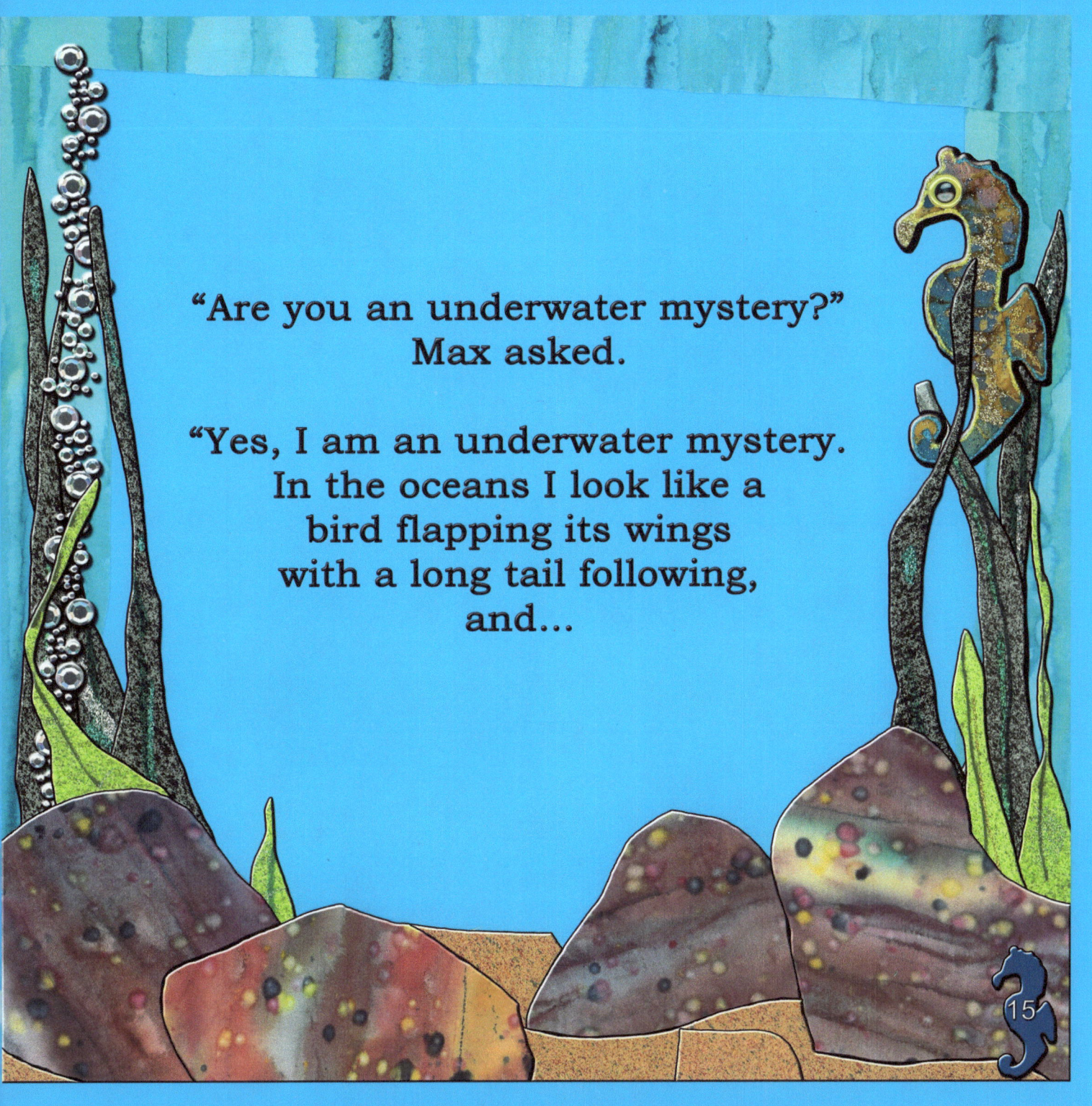

"Are you an underwater mystery?"
Max asked.

"Yes, I am an underwater mystery.
In the oceans I look like a
bird flapping its wings
with a long tail following,
and...

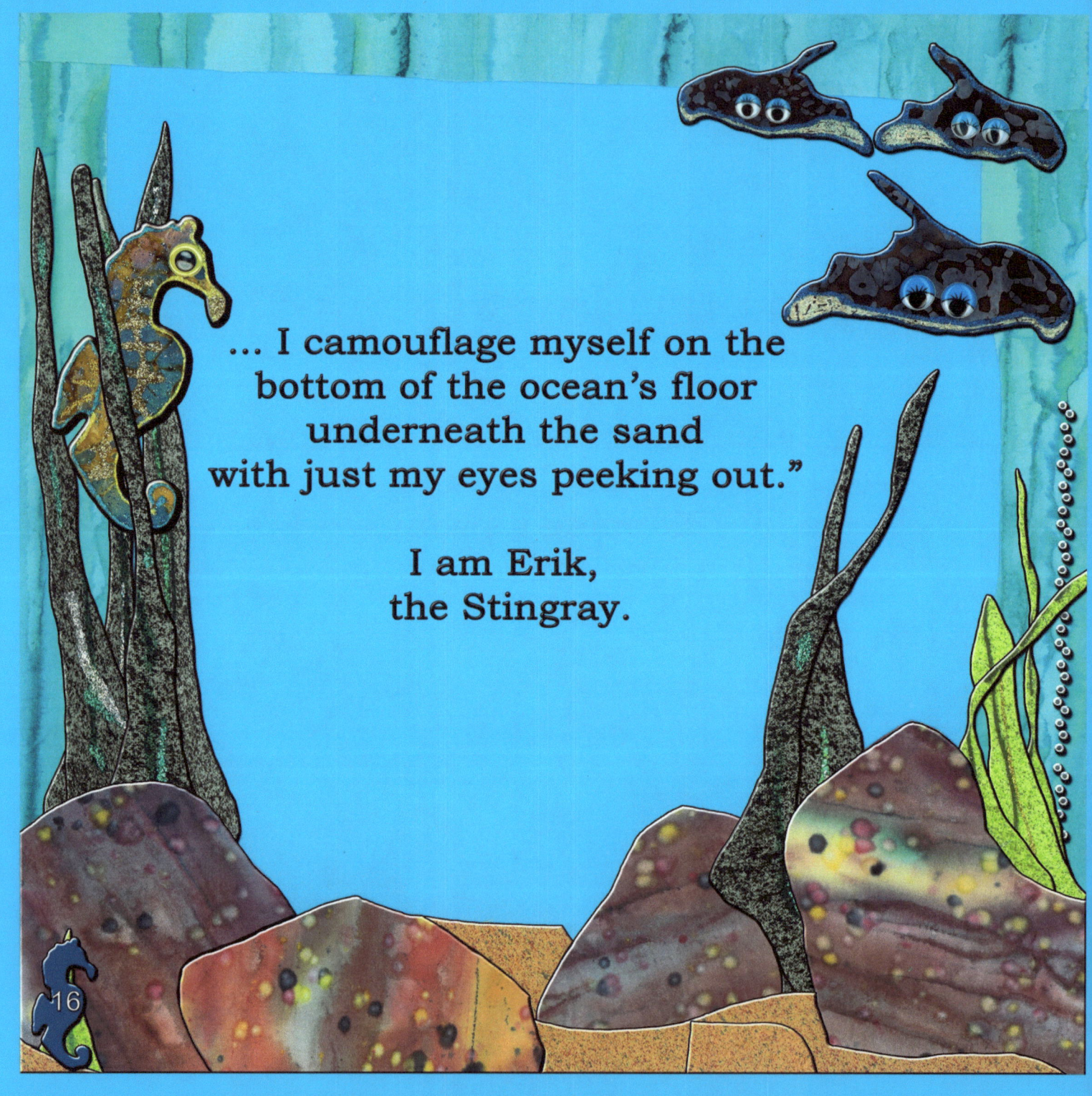

… I camouflage myself on the
bottom of the ocean's floor
underneath the sand
with just my eyes peeking out."

I am Erik,
the Stingray.

18

"Are you an underwater
mystery?"
Max asked.

"Yes, I am an underwater
mystery.
I am very social, playful,
and intelligent,
and...

...I am the largest of the dolphins and can swim up to 30 mph."

I am Mark, the Orca.

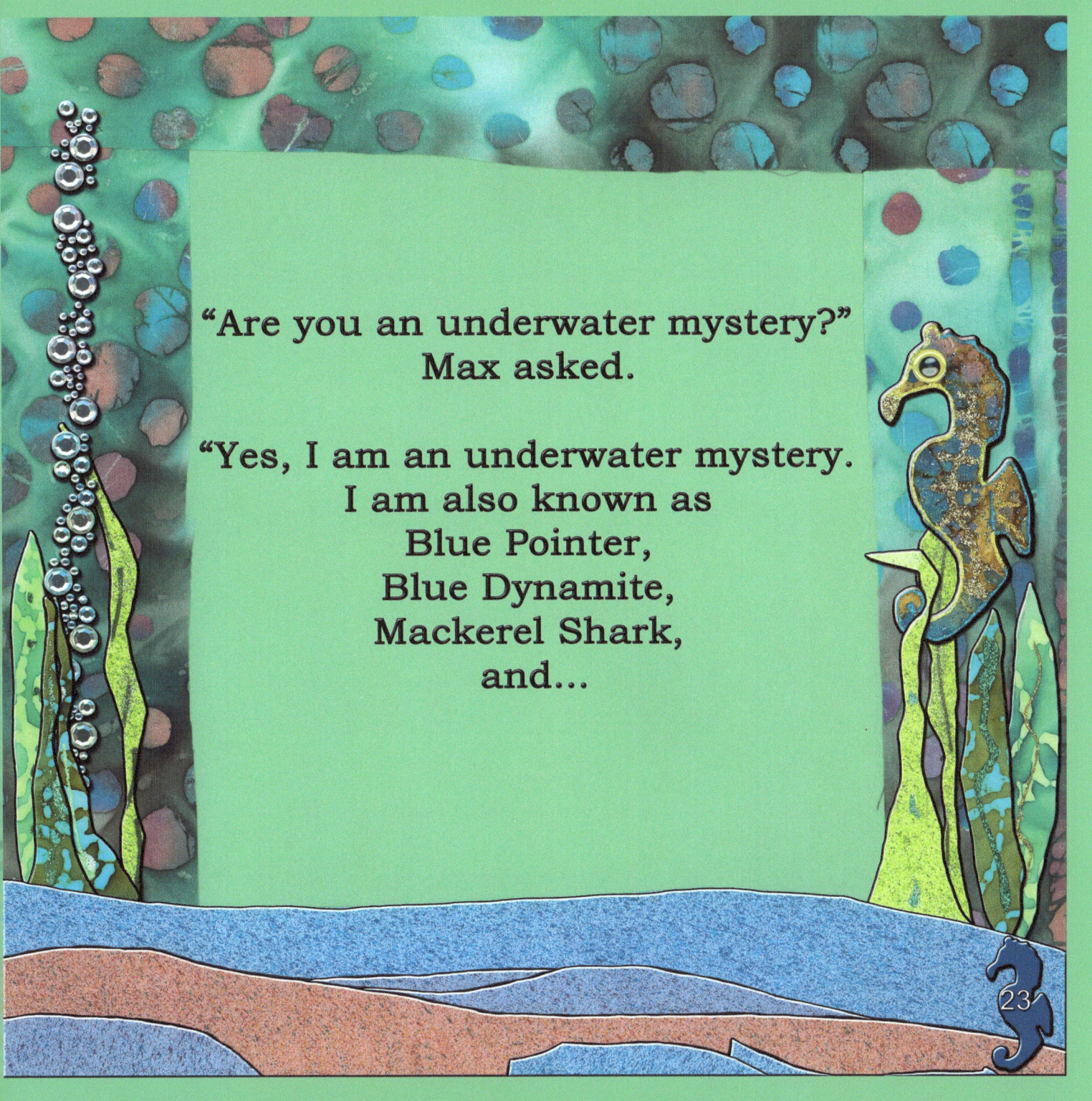

"Are you an underwater mystery?"
Max asked.

"Yes, I am an underwater mystery.
I am also known as
Blue Pointer,
Blue Dynamite,
Mackerel Shark,
and...

...I can swim 21 mph,
but in a short burst
I can go as fast as
50 mph!"

I am Joshua,
the Shortfin Mako Shark.

25

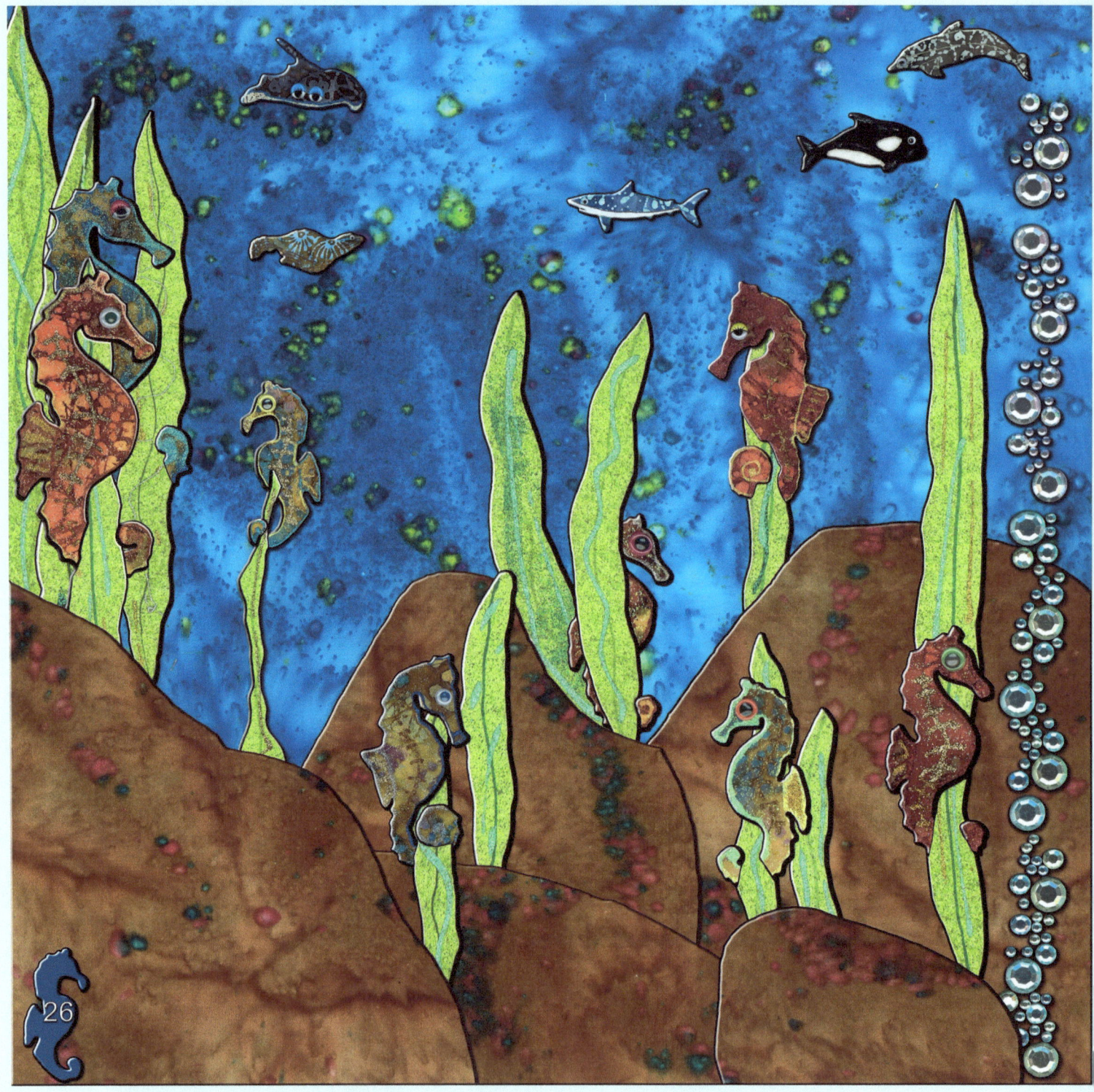
26

"So how was your underwater mystery adventure, my son?" Dad asked.

"I explored the oceans' waters, in between rocks, sand, and in many seaweed beds. I learned about five different types of sea creatures swimming nearby when I was on my adventure, Dad. I made five new friends today!" Max shouted.

27

"OK, OK, Max, settle down!

You can tell me all about it when I put you to bed,"

Dad said in his very loving voice.

29

Sea Creatures

The Bottlenose dolphin can live for 20 years, grow to 13 ft., and weigh up to 1,400 lbs. During the eight hour sleep cycle, the one side of the brain stays active and the other side becomes inactive.

The Harbor seal can live for 35 years, grow to 6 ft., and weigh up to 290 lbs. They rest on rocks, ice, and sandy spots near or on the coastlines. They can sleep underwater by their nostrils closing, but need to resurface frequently to breathe.

The Orca can live for 80 years, grow to 32 ft., and weigh up to 6 tons. An Orca's brain is about four times bigger than a human brain. There are four different types of Orcas, but all are similar in the way they look. Orcas are marine mammals and are apex predators, which mean are top predators.

The Seahorse can live for 5 years, grow to 14 in. and weigh up to 2 lbs. Their fins can beat up to 50 times a second but seahorses move slowly and are bad swimmers. The male seahorse carries the eggs in its pouch before they hatch into baby seahorses. They do not have stomachs or teeth, so food passes quickly through their bodies.

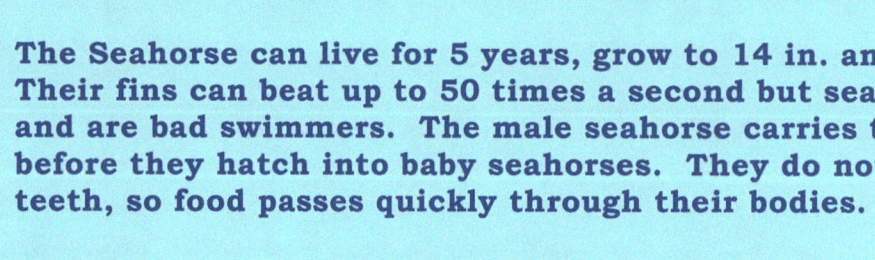

The Shortfin Mako shark can live for 30 years, grow to 13 ft., and weigh up to 1,220 lbs. They can swim down to 490 ft. They can be found in cool or warm waters all over the world's oceans.

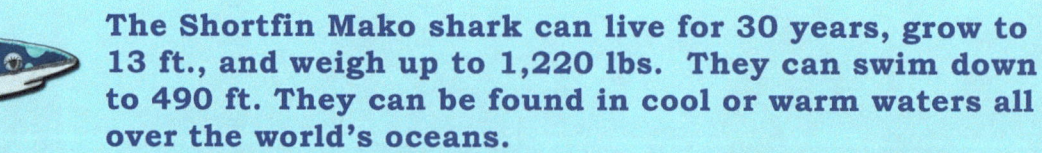

The Stingray can live for 25 years, grow to 6.5 ft., and weigh up to 790 lbs. They live in shallow warm waters and most of the time are inactive and stay buried in the sand. They do not use their eyes to hunt their prey; instead they use smell and electroreceptors.

Dedication:
    Cheryl Sorochynskyj and Max

Acknowledgement:
    Thank you to Susan Fourgerel and Gerri Post who helped edit this book.

Inspiration:
    One day a boy named Max, said to another person, "Are you an underwater mystery?" I heard that and I thought to myself, I can write a children's picture book using that question. And that is how this story started. Then, I decided to answer the question by, "Yes, I am an underwater mystery," followed by an explanation.

    My pictures were inspired by my close friend Cheryl. Cheryl found a big box filled to the rim with colorful fabrics. She saved the box for me. When I saw the fabric, I could see all the many different types of sea creatures that live in the ocean. As all of the bright colorful fabrics surrounded me, I felt as if I were swimming in the depths of the ocean with all the ocean life around me.

About the Author:
    Jacquelyn received her B.S. in Psychology from UMass, Amherst and her M.S. in Childhood Education and Childhood Special Education from LIU.

    She loves to write, draw, read lots of books, photograph the world around her, and spend as much time with her family and close friends as possible.

Other Books:
    Butterfly Haiku

Contact: **jfourgerel@gmail.com**

Website: **jacquelynjaiefourgerel.com**

Max's Underwater Mystery! #1: Exploring the Oceans

Written and Illustrated by Jacquelyn Jaie Fourgerel

Copyright: 2014 Jacquelyn Jaie Fourgerel. All Rights Reserved.

Technical and Graphic Editing by: Susan Fourgerel

ISBN-13: 978-1508453734

ISBN-10: 150845373X

Printed by: CreateSpace an Amazon Company 2015

"Hope you join me on my next adventure exploring the oceans' sea creatures!

Max's Underwater Mystery! #2: Adventures in the Oceans.

See you soon!"